THE Baby Cuisine

COOKBOOK

THE Baby Cuisine
COOKBOOK

Internationally inspired organic recipes
for babies from **6** to **18** months

SHANE VALENTINE
With Dr. Tamara Cullen, ND

ISBN-10: 0-615-30233-5
ISBN-13: 978-0-615-30233-1

www.alinascucina.com

Information found in this book, whether provid-
ed by Alina's Cucina, its contributors, licensors
or users, is for informational purposes only and
is not intended to be a substitute for professional
medical or dietary treatment. Just like adults,
every child is unique and a diet should reflect
that. Always consult with your child's physician
or a qualified health care provider before deciding
on your child's diet.

contents

introduction

Seeing this cookbook come to life takes me back to the beginning of this journey, when Alina first started eating solids and we began introducing her to the many amazing flavors of the world. At that point I knew what I wanted for Alina, but I certainly didn't know it would lead me here. Although I had been to culinary school, I was a dad, just like other dads, who wanted the very best for my child.

Knowing that a child's palate is developed by the time they are two, I wanted to broaden Alina's experience of food early so she could enjoy eating as much as her mother and I do. And, like all parents, I wanted what was best for her health. That meant giving her fresh, flavorful food that was full of nutrients and devoid of preservatives, fillers, excess sugar and salt.

But all the baby food recipes I found sounded so uninspired, and tasted just the same. How could I feed this food to Alina if I could barely eat it myself?

I started wondering what parents around the world feed their babies. And then I started asking them. Through many conversations, parents from France, Thailand, Brazil and beyond told me the same thing: their babies eat what the rest of the family eats. This was not only my hunch, but what I really wanted for Alina all along. I headed straight to the kitchen and got busy testing recipes.

To make sure I was covering all the appropriate nutritional bases, I consulted with Dr. Tamara Cullen, Seattle's leading naturopathic family physician specializing in pediatrics. At first, Dr. Cullen advised me on the appropriate age to introduce each new recipe to Alina. Once it became clear that my passion was blooming into a full-fledged family business, Dr. Cullen joined the team as our medical advisor and has now put her seal of approval on every recipe in this book.

My hope is that this cookbook will make life easier and tastier for your entire family. All of these recipes are so flavorful, your whole family will love them. That means more quality time together at the kitchen table, which I believe is one of the best ways to give your little one a healthy, happy start in life.

From my kitchen to yours - enjoy, have fun, and eat well!

the first six months

In the first six months of baby's life, there is no doubt that breastmilk is best. Studies have conclusively shown that breastmilk is composed of everything a baby needs to develop a strong immune system and a healthy digestive tract.[1] It's easily dispensed by mom, easily absorbed by baby, and there is no waste, no clean-up, and no need to sterilize. Studies have recently shown another advantage to breastmilk: the flavor of breastmilk changes depending on what mom eats, so baby is exposed to a much wider palate of tastes than babies who are formula fed. Through breastfeeding, moms can minimize the "picky-eater-syndrome" that's so common during babyhood and early childhood.[2]

Women who are unable to breastfeed can still take steps to expand baby's palate from a very early age. By following these recipes your baby will be eating diverse and flavorful foods beginning at six months. Watch your baby's taste buds come alive.

teaching healthy eating habits

Babies learn everything through modeling and who better to model healthy eating habits than parents! Take your baby to the local farmers' markets or the grocery store and let them smell and touch the produce. Talk to them about the foods and explain why you are buying those yummy carrots. How fun for kids to see what food looks like when it comes out of the earth! For example, carrots are long and tapered at the tips, and a little dirty with tall greens sprouting out of the tops—very different from baby carrots kids often see in their lunches at school. Explain why you are choosing to buy organic products and why they are good for the world. Children are truly like sponges and they love to learn. Eating in season is especially easy when visiting the local farmers' markets or joining a community supported agriculture (CSA) farm. Food provides just the right nutritional balance when eaten in season.

Try to feed your baby organically grown foods when possible. Certified organic means that there are no chemical pesticides or herbicides used on produce and no antibiotics or hormones given to the animals that produce food for us. In addition, these animals are fed grain that is organic. In the United States, the incidence of preventable diseases, like diabetes and cancer, is on the rise, and many authorities believe chemicals are partly to blame.[3] If we want to change the direction of our health, we need to start with what we use to fuel our bodies. The biggest drawback to shopping organic...the price-tag. Clearly organic foods are more expensive. If budget is a concern when shopping organic, consider buying meats, dairy and eggs first. Also, consider buying organic fruits and veggies where the skin is eaten. Simply washing non-organic fruits and vegetables can help as well. Please see www.EWG.org for more information.

Let's face it, as parents we have a lot of choices when it comes to how we feed our children. Fortunately, more and more parents are beginning to explore the benefits of homemade baby food. The thought of making baby food may seem daunting at first. Didn't our moms just pop open a jar? But we know that eating organic whole foods that are chemical and preservative-free leads to a decreased risk of chronic diseases, such as Parkinson's, cancer, heart disease, and diabetes.[4] By making homemade food for your baby, you are giving him/her the best start in life you can imagine. Plus, it's easier than you might think! We'll show you just how easy it can be.

starting solid foods

Most babies are ready to begin solid foods around six months of age. A number of other factors that show readiness are timed accordingly. Baby should: have at least one tooth so that the salivary enzymes are stimulated in the mouth for digestion;[5] be able to sit up with support and have strong neck and back muscles; be able to open his/her mouth and work his/her tongue to take the food in, rather than pushing it back out; be able to swallow well without gagging on the food and be interested in eating. With all of these developments in place, baby eats very well the first time s/he tries solid foods and you can feel confident in knowing their body is ready. It is a good idea to introduce a single food at a time; one that is pureed, easy to digest, and not too acidic. Most new moms hear from friends and family to start solid feedings with rice cereal, that this is the best first food. Current research shows us differently.[6] Grains are actually more difficult to digest than fruits, vegetables and even meats. Instead of a bland cereal, make sure your baby's first foray into food is special. Try a vegetable or fruit that is in season! Some of our favorites include squash, sweet potato, applesauce, pears, peaches and banana. (Table 1).

*Table 1 – *Indicates more highly allergic food*

6 Months		9 Months		12 Months		15 Months
· applesauce	· brown rice	· blueberries	· corn*	· strawberries*	· fish	· pineapple
· pear	· quinoa	· raspberries	· barley*	· grapes	· beef	· orange (citrus)*
· peach	· millet	· melon	· rye*	· dates	· pork	· honey
· nectarine	· flax oil	· chard	· amazake	· raisins	· cow's milk yogurt & cheeses*	· peppers
· plum	· olive oil	· kale	· thinned almond butter*	· artichokes	· onions	· peanut butter*
· avocado	· safflower oil	· bok choy	· thinned seed butters	· nori		
· banana	· sunflower oil	· asparagus	· maple syrup	· mushrooms		
· carrots	· goat's milk	· celery	· blackstrap molasses	· cashew butter		
· sweet potato		· cucumbers	· goat's milk yogurt & cheese	· macadamia nut butter		
· yams		· green beans	· lamb	· whole seeds		
· beets		· beans (black, pinto, etc.)	· garlic*	· buckwheat		
· peas		· eggplant		· spelt*		
· zucchini		· cabbage		· wheat*		
· parsnips		· broccoli		· tomatoes*		
· winter squashes		· cauliflower		· soy*		
· chicken		· potato		· eggs*		
· turkey		· oatmeal*				

This table is a rough guide and does not have to be followed strictly based on the baby's age, but more by the baby's tolerance.

Separate the introduction of each new food by three to four days to see if baby has any sort of reactions that may indicate an allergy or intolerance. These may include runny nose, congestion, diarrhea, constipation, diaper rash, skin rash, green mucousy stools, fussiness or difficulty sleeping. If foods are introduced too closely together, these reactions may be missed and it becomes more difficult to discern which foods may be causing a reaction. When a food is introduced and no negative reaction is seen, feel confident in adding that food to the baby's repertoire in addition to the new foods. Within one month, you will have a repertoire of safe foods.

Now you can start experimenting with recipes. Don't be afraid to add spices or just a dash of salt or natural sugar to enhance flavors. Our recipes will help guide you as all have appropriate ages listed for their ingredients. If there is a food reaction, leave that food out for another month or so and then try it again. If baby still reacts, wait about three more months before trying again. Most recipes will have substitutes listed for those babies who have allergies, so you can still experiment with flavors. Remember, the first six months of solid foods are all about trying new tastes and textures. In the beginning baby may only want about one tablespoon of solid food per day, but you may give more if s/he likes it! Always end the meal with breastmilk or formula to make sure baby gets all of their nutrition needs.

Once baby is eating primarily solid foods, most meals should consist of a healthy balance of protein, good fats, and complex carbohydrates. Protein helps with growing bodies and strong muscles; good fats (balanced in omega 3, 6, and 9 fatty acids) help growing brains and nervous systems; and complex carbohydrates provide sustained energy throughout the day. (See Table 2 for examples of proteins, omega 3, 6, 9 fats and complex carbohydrates.) A balance of these foods allows babies to reach optimal growth and development.

Table 2

Protein	Omega-3 fats	Omega-6 fats	Omega-9 fats	Complex carbs
· meat · fish · dairy · eggs · nuts/seeds · legumes	· flaxseed · coldwater fish	· sunflower oil · safflower oil · canola oil	· olive oil	· brown rice · quinoa · millet · oats · polenta · barley

In the six to nine month period, solid foods should be accompanied by breastmilk or formula, but by nine months, you may begin to introduce pure water. Most babies should drink about one-quarter of their body weight in ounces per day–so a twenty pound baby would drink five ounces of water. Babies can start having cow's milk around twelve months (see section on food intolerance). At this age, serve the milk after the solids foods or in between meals, so baby doesn't fill up on milk before eating. Juice should be thought of as a treat and served in limited quantities. Without the fiber of the fruit, the juice consists solely of simple carbohydrates and it's very sweet. Cut the juice's sugar in half by diluting with water. The less exposure your baby has to sugars now, the better for your baby in the long run.

By nine to twelve months, babies are encouraged to be eating three meals per day of solid foods. The volume will depend on your baby's appetite and may even change from day to day. Serve a variety of colorful foods to help ensure consumption of appropriate vitamins and minerals for optimum growth and development. Think of the foods as a rainbow; each natural color of fruits and vegetables is providing specific nutrients.

special diets

Vegetarianism – a vegetarian diet can be perfectly healthy for babies, but it may take some extra thought to ensure enough protein, iron and vitamin B-12 are being eaten. Vegetarian proteins should be combined to provide a complete protein. (See Table 3) With veganism (which includes avoidance of all animal products including dairy and eggs), extra special care must be taken. In addition to protein, iron and B-12, focus should be given to vegan calcium sources. Please see Table 4 for a list of vegetarian iron, B-12 and calcium.

Table 3 – Vegetarian protein

A Grain + A Legume		Nuts/Seeds	Dairy	Eggs
· rice	· beans	· sunflower	· goat's milk	· chicken
· quinoa	· lentils	· sesame	· sheep's milk products	· quail
· millet	· peas	· pumpkin	· cow's milk	· duck
· oats	· peanuts	· flax		
· nuts	· soy	· almonds		
· wheat		· cashews		
· spelt		· macadamias		
· barley		· pistachios		
· rye		· pecans		
		· walnuts		

Table 4

Vegetarian Iron	Vegetairan B-12	Vegan Calcium
· spinach	· seaweeds (nori)	· white beans
· raisins	· spirulina	· almonds
· dark leafy greens	· chlorella	· dark leafy greens
· prunes		· tofu
· blackstrap molasses		· blackstrap molases
· soybeans		· fortified orange juice
· lentils		· okra
· quinoa		· bok choy
· beans		· sesame
· potatoes		· broccoli
· sesame		· onions
· peas		· soy

Pescevegetarians include fish and shellfish in their diets. Seafood is an excellent source of protein and nutrients, but can be allergenic as well. Care should be taken to avoid shellfish until twelve months of age, or later if there is a family history of shellfish allergy. White fish can also be allergenic, but less often. While fish has many beneficial components (protein, essential fatty acids like omega-3's, iron, potassium and calcium), it can also contain potentially toxic levels of mercury and PCB's[7]. A conscientious consumer of fish must also reckon with the truth that certain members of the ocean's bounty have been overfished, leading to problems with the ocean food chain and contributing to the detriment of the environment[8]. (See Table 5)

Table 5 – data from www.nrdc.org

Mercury Levels in Fish			Overfished
High	Medium	Low	
· bluefish	· bass *(striped, black)*	· anchovies	· marlin
· grouper	· carp	· calamari	· orange roughy
· mackeral *(king, spanish, gulf)*	· cod *(alaskan)*	· catfish	· seabass
· marlin	· halibut *(pacific, atlantic)*	· clam	· shark
· orange roughy	· lobster	· cod (artic)	· swordfish
· seabass *(chilean)*	· mahi mahi	· crab (domestic)	· tilefish
· shark	· monkfish	· crafish/crayfish	· ahi tuna
· swordfish	· perch *(freshwater)*	· flounder	· yellowfin tuna
· tilefish	· sablefish	· haddock (atlantic)	· atlantic halibut
· tuna *(ahi, yellowfin, bigeye, canned albacore)*	· skate	· hake	· monkfish
	· snapper	· herring	· skate
	· tuna *(canned chunk light, skiplight)*	· mackeral (n. atlantic, chub)	· snapper
	· sea trout	· mullet	· skipjack tuna
		· oyster	· flounder
		· perch (ocean)	· haddock
		· plaice	· scallop
		· pollock	· grouper
		· salmon	
		· sardine	
		· scallop	
		· sole (pacific)	
		· tilapia	
		· trout (freshwater)	
		· whitefish	
		· whiting	

children with allergies

The incidence of food allergies in children is increasing. In addition, we have learned that many children experience food intolerances which may not cause classic allergic symptoms, but still affect the child.[9] Speak with your doctor if you are especially concerned about your child based on their personal or family history of food allergies. In general, food allergies can cause asthma, eczema, rhinitis (chronic runny nose and congestion), hives and anaphylaxis. Food intolerances can cause constipation, diarrhea, muscle aches, joint pains, headaches, congestion, fatigue and rashes. If you discover that your child is allergic or intolerant to a food, please use Appendix A for help with recipe substitutions.

storing baby food

Once you have made a delicious batch of food for your baby, store it properly for future use. An ice cube tray works well to portion out the foods in individual servings. Put the tray in a freezer bag to protect the nutrients from the cold so they don't break down quite as fast. These foods will last at least two months in the freezer. If the homemade baby food is stored in the refrigerator, it will last two to three days in a well-sealed container if the refrigerator temperature is maintained at 40° degrees Fahrenheit. Pyrex (glass) storage containers are readily available in various sizes and are preferable to plastic so no dangerous chemicals like PCB's, BPA's or xenoestrogens are leached into the food. These compounds have been shown to disrupt homone production[10] and potentially lead to cancer and metabolic disorders.[11] Once baby has eaten from a portion of food, it is best to throw it out. Bacteria are more likely to grow once saliva has mixed with the food.

reheating baby food

Reheating food is best done on the stove in a stainless steel or glass pot or pan. The food may be thawed in the refrigerator if desired, but never on the counter. Leaving food out at room temperature too long can breed bacteria. Microwaving, while useful in a pinch, can heat food unevenly and cause hot spots in the food, which can burn baby's mouth. In addition, microwaving can deplete nutrients from the food.[12]

Now you have learned the basics, and have packed the pantry for the trip. Are you excited to begin cooking-round-the-world for your baby? Pick a country, learn some culture and start eating! Your baby will be an eager companion to your adventure.

Recipes

VGN	/	VEGAN
VGT	/	VEGETARIAN
GF	/	GLUTEN-FREE
DF	/	DAIRY-FREE

One of my favorite dishes growing up on Long Island, New York was Chicken Parmesan. I would run to the neighborhood pizzeria to get it – it was so good! Believe it or not, this is one of the first dishes I made for Alina and I am so thrilled to see her enjoy it as much as I do. I pureed this for Alina when she was around a year old, but it did not take long until I was able to cut it into small pieces for her to devour. I am honored to share with you Alina's Cucina's Signature Dish!

Buon appetito, bambino!

ALINA APPROVAL DPT.
ITALY

chicken parmesan

FOR BABIES: 12 Months +

1/3 CUP orzo pasta

4 OUNCES boneless, skinless chicken breast

1/8 CUP onion, chopped

1 CLOVE garlic, minced

1 TABLESPOON olive oil

1 1/4 CUP tomato sauce (15 ounce can)

1 TEASPOON fresh oregano, finely chopped

1 TEASPOON fresh basil, finely chopped

1/8 TEASPOON salt

fresh ground pepper

1 TABLESPOON grated parmesan cheese

1/4 CUP low moisture mozzarella, grated

01   Cook pasta according to instructions on box. Pasta should be soft, not firm. Reserve pasta water for pureeing.

02   Cut chicken breast into 1/4 inch slices, then cut in half to ensure even cooking.

03   Sauté onion and garlic in olive oil on medium heat until the onions are translucent, about 2-3 minutes.

04   Add tomato sauce, oregano, basil, salt and pepper. Simmer on medium/low heat for 4-5 minutes. Add chicken breast and increase heat to medium. Simmer for 5-6 minutes until the chicken is cooked.

05   Remove from heat and stir in cooked orzo, parmesan, and mozzarella.

06   For younger babies, puree with hand blender or in food processor fitted with steel blade. Use reserved pasta water 1/4 cup at a time to achieve desired consistency.

07   Freeze pureed mixture in ice cube trays for up to 2 months or store in the refrigerator for up to 3 days.

Makes 2 cups.

Nestled between Florence, Milan and Venice lies the Emilia-Romagna Region of Northern Italy, from which Bolognese sauce originated, named for the region's capital, Bologne. Bolognese sauce is quintessential Italian farmhouse cooking; a hearty sauce made with farm-fresh meats, cream and wine. I have adjusted it ever-so-slightly for baby, using ground turkey meat which is one of the easiest meats for babies to digest. Serve this on its own or with small-shaped pasta, such as orzo.

FOR BABIES: 9 Months + or 12 Months + if served with pasta

turkey bolognese

ALINA APPROVAL DPT.

ITALY

1/8 CUP onion, chopped

1 CLOVE garlic, minced

1 TABLESPOON olive oil

1 1/4 CUP tomato sauce

1 TEASPOON fresh oregano,
finely chopped

1 TEASPOON fresh basil,
finely chopped

1/8 TEASPOON sea salt

fresh ground pepper

1/3 POUND ground turkey breast

01   On medium heat, sauté onion and garlic
in olive oil until the onion is translucent.
About 2-3 minutes.

02   Add tomato sauce, oregano, basil, salt and
pepper. Simmer on medium/low heat for
4-5 minutes.

03   Add ground turkey breast and increase heat
to medium. Simmer for 4-5 minutes until
the turkey is cooked through.

04   For a finer consistency, puree sauce using
a hand blender or food processor fitted with
a steel blade.

05   Keep in refrigerator for up to 3 days or
freeze in ice cube trays for up to 2 months.

Makes 3/4 cup.

Close your eyes and imagine the pleasure of tasting fruit's intensely sweet flavors for the first time. Your baby's palate is untouched by high fructose corn syrup or processed sugars, so let him/her taste fruit with all its natural sweetness. And when organic fruit is available and in season – I would bet NOTHING tastes better. Serve one of the suggested purees below, combine fruits to create your own puree, or use a puree as part of another recipe, such as the Fruit Parfait. Always try to use fruit that is organic, local and in-season for a winning combination.

ALINA APPROVAL DPT.

FRANCE

AC 068

pureed fruit

FOR BABIES: **6** Months **+** except berries wait until **9** months

TYPES OF FRUIT TO TRY:

Strawberry	Raspberry
Banana	Kiwi
Mango	Apple
Blueberry	Pear

PREPARATION

01   Strawberry- Puree 1 pound of strawberries using a hand blender or food processor.

02   Banana - Use hand blender to puree 1 large banana.

03   Mango - With the peel still on, cut the mango in halves, being careful not to cut into the pit. Working with one half at a time, score the mango (do not cut through the peel) making a checkerboard pattern. Using a spoon, scoop out the flesh. Using a hand blender, puree mango chunks.

04   Blueberry - Puree 1 or 2 cartons of blueberries using a hand blender or food processor.

05   Raspberry- Puree 1 or 2 cartons of raspberries using a hand blender or food processor.

06   Kiwi - Using a vegetable peeler, peel 5 kiwi. Slice kiwi, then cut the green flesh away from the white seeded center. Puree green flesh with a hand blender.

07   Apple - Peel 2 apples and use a fine microplane to shred the apple being careful not to shred the seeds.

08   Pear - Peel 2 pears and use a fine microplane to shred the pear being careful not to shred the seeds.

A deliciously healthy sweet-treat! Yogurt is not only convenient food for babies, but also contains live probiotic cultures that are beneficial to your baby's digestive track. The addition of flaxseed oil adds omega-3 fatty acids that are important for nerve cell development. Use fresh or pureed fruit to add more color and sweetness to the dish.

FOR BABIES: **7** Months + with goat milk yogurt

12 Months + with cow milk yogurt

yogurt parfaits

1/8 CUP - 1/2 CUP plain or vanilla whole milk yogurt
(depending on baby's appetite)

1 TEASPOON flaxseed oil

1/8 CUP- 1/2 CUP fresh fruit, pureed or chopped

01 In a bowl, mix yogurt and flaxseed oil with a spoon until oil is well incorporated.

02 Depending on the amount of yogurt used, add equal portion of chopped or pureed fruit to yogurt.

Makes 1 serving.

ALINA APPROVAL DPT.

FRANCE

AC 068

Carrots are super sweet when pureed, and here I add tarragon, an herb typically used in French cooking, which only enhances that naturally sweet flavor. Babies, quite simply, adore their carrots!

Allez, mange mon petit ange.
– Eat my little angel.

ALINA APPROVAL DPT.

FRANCE

AC 068

tarragon carrots

FOR BABIES: **6** Months **+**

VGN / VGT / GF / DF

7 carrots, peeled and roughly chopped

1/8 CUP fresh tarragon, chopped

1/2 CUP water

01 Steam carrots for approximately 15 minutes, until fork tender.

02 Using a hand blender or food processor fitted with steel blade, puree carrots, tarragon, and 1/4 cup water.

03 Continue to blend, adding in remaining water as necessary. For older babies, use less water and do not puree as finely.

04 Servings may be frozen in ice cube trays for up to 2 months.

Makes about 2 cups.

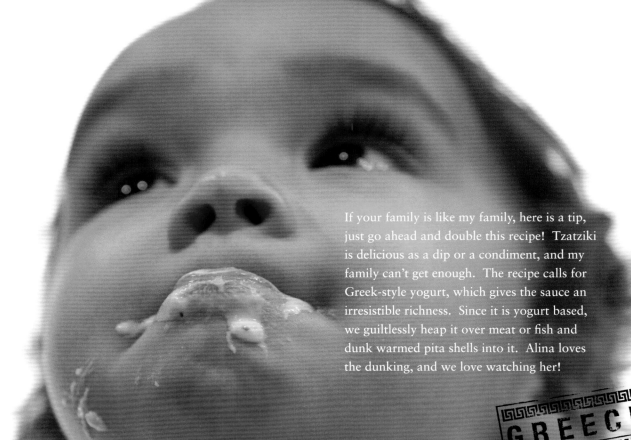

If your family is like my family, here is a tip, just go ahead and double this recipe! Tzatziki is delicious as a dip or a condiment, and my family can't get enough. The recipe calls for Greek-style yogurt, which gives the sauce an irresistible richness. Since it is yogurt based, we guiltlessly heap it over meat or fish and dunk warmed pita shells into it. Alina loves the dunking, and we love watching her!

GREECE
ALINA APPROVAL

tzatziki

FOR BABIES: 7 Months + with goat milk yogurt
12 Months + with cow milk yogurt

1 MEDIUM english cucumber, peeled

1 CUP goat milk yogurt or plain whole milk greek style yogurt

1 SMALL garlic clove, minced

7-8 fresh mint leaves, chopped

1 TABLESPOON fresh dill, chopped

1/8 TEASPOON sea salt

fresh ground pepper to taste

01   Seed the cucumber by slicing in half lengthwise. Using a spoon, scrape out seeds and discard.

02   Grate the cucumber with a medium grater. Squeeze grated cucumber in a clean kitchen towel, removing as much moisture as possible.

03   Combine the cucumber, yogurt, garlic, mint leaves, dill, salt and pepper into bowl and mix with a spoon. Alternatively, you may also mix in a food processor or with a hand blender to get a finer consistency.

04   Note: If you cannot find Greek yogurt, try finding European style yogurt. If neither are available or if you are using Goat Milk yogurt, do the following to achieve the thick style yogurt:

05   Put a colander lined with a piece of white paper towel or cheese cloth over a bowl.

06   Pour 1 cup of yogurt into the lined colander. Refrigerate for 1-2 hours. The liquid will slowly drain through the paper towel to the bowl underneath the colander.

07   After draining, follow above recipe.

08   Tzatziki can be stored in refrigerator for up to 3 days. Freezing not recommended.

Makes 1 1/2 cups.

gyro

FOR BABIES: **7** Months + *if finely chopped*
9 Months + *if larger chop or sliced*

Whether in Athens or Astoria, Queens, NY, – a Gyro (pronounced "yee-roh") is one of the quintessential dishes in Greek cuisine. It is traditionally a sandwich filled with spit-roasted lamb. I love the fresh aromatic Greek flavors, so I created this baby-friendly version for you – minus the sandwich part. This recipe is easily doubled and can be served to the whole family. It is delicious with Tzatziki and warm pita.

When gathered around the table eating this dish together, teach your baby that "S'aga po" means "I love you" in Greek.

1/2 POUND ground lamb

1 SMALL CLOVE garlic, minced

1 TEASPOON onion, finely chopped

1/2 TEASPOON fresh mint, finely chopped

1/2 TEASPOON fresh marjoram, finely chopped

1/2 TEASPOON fresh oregano, finely chopped

1/8 TEASPOON sea salt

fresh ground pepper

olive oil

01   Preheat oven to 350 degrees. Lightly grease muffin pan with olive oil.

02   Combine ground lamb, garlic, onion, mint, marjoram, oregano, salt and pepper until well mixed.

03   Divide mixture into three portions. Fill muffin tin with each portion, packing the muffin tin but not over filling them.

04   Place muffin tin in a shallow water bath and bake for 30-45 minutes or until internal temperature is 170 - 175 degrees.

05   Place gyro onto a rack to set for 10 minutes.

06   To serve, finely chop meat or slice meat for older babies.

07   Gyro will keep in the fridge for 3 days, or freeze the rest for up to 2 months.

Makes 3 muffin size patties.

Offer your baby a taste of the exotic Middle East and at the same time, introduce beans, with Hummus. Beans offer an additional protein source for your baby. You can blend it up in minutes and little hands will be delighted to dip into its smooth, creamy texture. Serve this with the gyro, tzatziki and warm pita for a complete Mediterranean meal.

Note to parents: bring it as a dip to your next party – it is that good and nobody will believe you when you say it is baby food!

hummus

FOR BABIES: **7** Months +

E LEBANON
ALINA APPROVAL DPT.

01 Rinse and drain the garbanzo beans in very cold water for 1 minute, as this helps dispel the gases for baby.

02 Using a hand blender or food processor fitted with a steel blade, mix until well combined, garbanzo beans, olive oil, lemon juice, garlic, salt and water, about 1 minute. Stop occasionally to scrape down sides of bowl.

03 Serve at room temperature.

04 Can be stored in refrigerator for up to 3 days. You may need to add more water after storage to create desired consistency for your baby. Freezing not recommended.

Makes about 2 cups.

1 CAN garbanzo beans
(**15** ounce)

1/4 CUP olive oil

juice of 1/2 a lemon

1 SMALL CLOVE
of garlic, whole

1/4 TEASPOON sea salt

1/4 CUP water

As this stew simmers on your stove, enjoy its decidedly Moroccan smells; turmeric, coriander, and cinnamon. This is a fabulous vegetarian meal for the whole family (it makes 7 cups!) and is rich in vitamin A (butternut squash), protein (garbanzo beans), complex carbohydrates (sweet potato), and fiber (apricots). Follow Moroccan tradition and serve it over couscous; you may share a good laugh as your baby practices utensil skills. We did!

ALINA APPROVAL DEPARTMENT
MOROCCO
AC•P

moroccan vegetable stew
with couscous

FOR BABIES: 7 Months + without couscous
12 Months + with couscous

1 TABLESPOON olive oil

1/4 onion, diced

1 TEASPOON turmeric

1 TEASPOON dry coriander

1 TEASPOON cinnamon

1/8 TEASPOON salt

fresh ground pepper

1 CUP carrot, shredded

1 CUP sweet potato, diced

2 CUPS butternut squash, diced

4 CUPS low sodium vegetable broth

1 CUP eggplant, peeled and diced

1 CUP zucchini, diced

1/4 CUP dried apricots, chopped

2 15 OZ CANS garbanzo beans, drained and rinsed

1 CUP dry couscous

01 In a large pot, heat olive oil on medium heat. Add onions and sauté until translucent, about 2-3 minutes.

02 Add turmeric, coriander, cinnamon, salt and pepper. Sauté with the onions until onions are coated.

03 Add carrot, sweet potato, butternut squash and 2 cups of the vegetable broth. Stir well to combine with onions and spices. Bring to a boil and then cover and reduce to low. Simmer for 15 minutes.

04 Add the eggplant, zucchini, apricots, garbanzo beans, and remaining 2 cups of vegetable broth. Bring back to a boil, cover and reduce to low. Simmer for 15-20 minutes, until the vegetables are tender.

05 Prepare the couscous according to the package instructions.

06 For younger babies, puree vegetable stew in a food processor fitted with a steel blade or with a hand blender.

07 Serve the stew as is, or over the couscous for babies 12 months and up.

08 Keep in refrigerator for up to 3 days or freeze left-overs in ice cube trays for up to 2 months.

Makes 7 cups.

Every country seems to have its own version of grilled meat on a skewer and Beef Satay is a typical Southeast Asian dish. I capture its essence while providing a full flavor experience for your little one. The combination of sweet coconut milk, fragrant lemongrass and zestful ginger really opens Alina's senses to this region of the world. And, of course, I got rid of the skewers!

beef satay

FOR BABIES: 7 Months +

ALINA APPROVAL DEPART.
AP 68   AP 68
THAILAND

1/4 POUND beef tenderloin

3/4 CUP coconut milk

1/4 CUP fresh cilantro, finely chopped

1/2 TEASPOON turmeric

1/2 TEASPOON lemongrass*, grated

1/8 TEASPOON fresh ginger, grated

01   Slice beef into 1/4 inch strips.

02   Whisk together coconut milk, cilantro, turmeric, lemongrass and ginger. Marinate beef in mixture in a non-reactive dish (like glass) for one hour in refrigerator.

03   On medium heat, simmer all ingredients for 10 minutes.

04   Puree and serve for younger babies, or cut beef into small bites for older babies.

Freeze in ice cube trays for up to 2 months or keep in the fridge up to 3 days.

Makes 1 1/4 cups.

*Working with lemongrass - Lemongrass has long, thin, light green leaves that overlap similar to a leek or scallion. Inside is a woody stem that is mostly white.

To use, trim away the green outer leaves exposing the white pale center. This is the only part used for cooking. Lemongrass can be grated as in this recipe, or it can be used whole and removed before serving

Our friend, Sonia Manhas, donated Khichri, a favorite family recipe, to Alina's Cucina.. Described as an Indian comfort food, turmeric helps aid with digestion. Pronounced "kitch-a-ree," it is a simple combination of lentils and rice and provides an excellent vegetarian source of protein and carbohydrates. I can whip this up in a jiffy for Alina, and I know you can too for your little one.

khichri

FOR BABIES: 7 Months +

ALINA APPROVAL DPT.

INDIA

ACP

1/2 CUP yellow lentils

1/2 CUP basmati rice

3 CUPS water

1/4 TEASPOON ground turmeric

1/4 TEASPOON sea salt

01 Combine lentils and rice in a medium sauce pan. Rinse the lentils and rice in three changes of water. Drain well.

02 Add water, bring to rapid boil, then reduce and simmer with the lid half on the pot.

03 Simmer for about 35-45 minutes until the khichri reaches a thick, soft consistency, stirring occasionally. It should be similar to risotto or grainy mashed potatoes. If the mixture absorbs the water and becomes dry, add more water and keep cooking.

04 Cool and serve, or puree in a food processor fitted with a steel blade or with a hand blender until desired consistency is reached.

05 Freeze leftovers in ice cube trays for up to 2 months or keep in the fridge for up to 3 days.

*If your baby is at least 12 months, a little butter & dollop of plain yogurt are excellent additions.

Makes about 3 cups.

guasacaca

My dear friend, Lilian Elias, was gracious enough to contribute her special recipe for Guasacaca, a salsa-like condiment from Venezuela that is usually served with meats or salads, but is also great for dipping pita, bread, or vegetables. Alina loves avocados, so this snack has been a huge hit with her. Make it a complete meal simply by serving it with chicken, beef, or another protein.

When you are feeding your baby, teach him/her to say "Gracias", "thank you" in Spanish.

VENEZUELA
ALINA APPROVAL DPT.
ENTRADA
PASSPORT AC

1 CUP avocado

1/4 CUP green bell pepper,
seeded and chopped

1/4 CUP red bell pepper,
seeded and chopped

1/4 CUP tomato,
seeded and chopped

1/3 CUP cilantro, chopped

1 scallion, chopped

1/4 CUP olive oil

juice of 1/2 a lime

1/8 TEASPOON sea salt

fresh ground pepper

01   Using a food processor or hand blender, combine all ingredients and blend until smooth, about 2 minutes. Stop occasionally to scrape down sides of bowl. The mixture should have the consistency of creamy peanut butter.

02   This dish cannot be frozen but will last in the fridge for 3 days, if it makes it that long!

Makes 1 1/2 cups.

El Savor de la Isla – The Flavor of the Island

Sofrito is the base used in virtually all Puerto Rican cooking, similar to the mirepoix used in France and the soffritto used in Italy. In all cases, the bases are blends of vegetables and herbs used to season cuisine, delivering the authentic flavors of their regions.

Sofrito is a combination of peppers and herbs, most often used to season legume and rice dishes, sauces, soups and stews. Traditionally, sofrito is made with recao (similar to cilantro) and aji dulce (a sweet habanero pepper). These two ingredients may be hard to find so this version uses cilantro and bell peppers instead. Trust me, it still captures the essence and flavor of the Island!

Once made, freeze your Sofrito in ice cube trays and save it to use in other Puerto Rican recipes, such as Puerto Rican Rice and Beans. It will be a huge convenience and will pack an authentic punch to your cooking that your family will savor.

Note – Sofrito is not meant to be eaten by itself, it is intended to be cooked with our other Puerto Rican recipes.

sofrito

FOR BABIES: **9** Months +

ALINA APPROVAL DPT.
PUERTO RICO
AC-P

1/2 MEDIUM tomato

1/4 green bell pepper, seeded

1/4 red bell pepper, seeded

2 LARGE garlic cloves

1/4 onion

1/2 BUNCH of cilantro

1 TEASPOON dried oregano

1 TABLESPOON canola oil

01   Combine all ingredients in a blender or food processor fitted with a steel blade. Blend until the mixture is smooth. Stop occasionally to scrape down sides of blender.

02   Freeze for up to 2 months in an ice cube tray for use in other recipes.

Makes 1 cup.

Rice and beans - a staple in kitchens around the world and soon to be a favorite for your family, too. Alina's Grandmother, 'Ama', helped me create this dish especially for Alina and she just loves it! This is an old family recipe and we've modified it so that all ages can enjoy it. The recipe calls for three cubes of Sofrito, which, if made ahead and frozen, will easily add authentic Puerto Rican flavors to your cooking.

Buen Provecho, bebita! Enjoy your meal, baby!

OR Que Rico! So good!

puerto rican
rice and beans

FOR BABIES: 9 Months +

1/2 CUP white rice

1/2 TEASPOON dried oregano

2 MEDIUM garlic cloves

1/2 TEASPOON salt

1/2 TEASPOON fresh ground pepper

3 CUBES of frozen sofrito

2 TABLESPOONS olive oil

3 CUPS water

1/2 CUP tomato sauce

1 CAN pinto beans, not drained (15 ounce)

01   Rinse the rice in three changes of cold water. Let the rice drain in colander over a bowl.

02   Using a mortar and pestle, mash the oregano, garlic, salt and pepper until they make a paste. Reserve 1 tablespoon of the paste, discard the rest.

03   In a medium sized pot, sauté oregano/garlic paste and sofrito (still frozen) in 1 tablespoon of olive oil on medium/low heat for 4 to 6 minutes.

04   Add water, tomato sauce and beans (with their liquid). Stir and increase heat to medium/high and bring to a boil, uncovered. When boiling, using a 1 cup measuring cup, remove 1 cup of the sauce from the top of the beans and reserve for blending.

05   Stir in the drained rice and remaining 1 tablespoon of olive oil. Cover pot and reduce heat to low. Cook for 20 minutes.

06   Stir rice and beans and recover. Continue cooking until rice is soft and moist, 10-20 minutes.

07   Remove from heat and cool.

08   Serve as is, or using a hand mixer or a food processor fitted with steel blade, add the 1 cup of reserved sauce and puree the rice and beans.

09   Can be stored in refrigerator for up to 3 days or freeze in ice cube trays for up to 2 months.

Makes 3 1/2 cups.

appendix a

Wheat flour substitutes: brown rice flour, tapioca flour, chickpea flour, oat flour (if not gluten sensitive), barley flour (if not gluten sensitive). For most recipes, replace 1 cup of wheat flour with 1 cup of oat or barley flour OR with 1/2 cup rice flour + 1/2 cup tapioca flour + 2 Tbsp. almond meal.

Gluten substitutes: brown rice flour, tapioca flour, chickpea flour (I don't typically recommend because of taste), quinoa flour. For most recipes, replace 1 cup wheat flour with 1/2 cup rice flour + 1/2 cup tapioca flour + 2 Tbsp. almond meal.

Dairy substitutes: soymilk, rice milk, oat milk, hemp milk, hazelnut milk (may be allergenic), almond milk (may be allergenic). For most recipes, replace 1 cup cow's milk with 1 cup plain alternative milk. Cheese substitutes are not recommended, as they all have casein in them, which can contribute to the allergic reaction.

Egg substitutes: In most recipes, replace 1 egg with 1 Tbsp. ground flax meal + 4 Tbsp. boiling water, whisk and let sit for 5-10 minutes.

Sugar substitutes: brown rice syrup, maple syrup, honey (if over 1 year), agave, stevia, banana or other fruit puree, sorghum, beet sugar.

Soy substitutes: other legumes (beans, peas, peanuts if tolerated), meats, other alternative milks.

footnotes

(1) Jackson, K. and Nazar A. (2006),"Breastfeeding, the Immune Response, and Long-term Health," JAOA Vol 106 No 4 (April 2006), pgs. 203-207

(2) Hausner, H., Bredie, W., Molgaard, C., Petersen, M., and Moller, P. (2008), "Differential transfer of dietary flavour compounds into human breast milk," Physiology & Behavior Vol. 95 Issues 1-2 (September 3, 2008), Pgs 118-124.

(3) Fiorini, K. (1998) "Industrial pollution, pesticides, and cancer," The Lancet, Vol. 352, issue 9144 (December 12, 1998), Page 1945.

(4) Habermann, B. (2001), "Growing Evidence of a Link Between Pesticides and Parkinson's Disease," Journal of Neuroscience Nursing, April 2001

Hardell L. and Eriksson M. (1999), "A Case-Control Study of Non-Hodgkin Lymphoma and exposure to Pesticides," CANCER Vol.85, No. 6 (March 15, 1999), pgs. 1353-1360

(5) de Almeida PDV, Grégio AMT, Machado MÂN, de Lima AAS, Azevedo LR. (2008), "Saliva Composition and Functions: A Comprehensive Review," J Contemp Dent Pract 2008 March; (9)3:072-080

(6) Poole JA; Barriga K; Leung DY; Hoffman M; Eisenbarth GS; Rewers M; Norris JM (2006), "Timing of initial exposure to cereal grains and the risk of wheat allergy," Pediatrics Vol. 117, No. 6 (2006) pgs. 2175-2182.

Krebs, N., Westcott JE; Butler N; Robinson C; Bell M (2006) "Meat as a first complementary food for breastfed infants: feasibility and impact on zinc intake and status." J Pediatr Gastroenterol Nutr. 42(2): (February 2006) pgs. 207-14.

(7) Burger, J.,; Stern, A., Gochfeld, M., (2005), "Mercury in Commercial Fish: Optimizing Individual Choices to Reduce Risk," Environ Health Perspect. 113(3): (2005) pgs. 266-271.

Judd N; Griffith WC; Faustman EM (2004), "Contribution of PCB exposure from fish consumption to total dioxin-like dietary exposure," Regul Toxicol Pharmacol; 40(2): (2004)1 pgs. 25-35.

(8) Coleman FC; Figueira WF; Ueland JS; Crowder LB (2004), "The impact of United States recreational fisheries on marine fish populations," Science 305(5692) (2004); pgs.1958-60.

(9) Sullivan PB_(1999), "Food allergy and food intolerance in childhood," Indian J Pediatr. 66(1 Suppl): (1999) S37-45.

(10) Rajapakse N; Silva E; Kortenkamp A (2002), "Combining xenoestrogens at levels below individual no-observed-effect concentrations dramatically enhances steroid hormone action," Environ Health Perspect. 110(9) (2002) pgs.917-921.

(11) vom Saal, FS., Myers, JP. (2008), "Bisphenol A and Risk of Metabolic Disorders,"

JAMA; 300(11): (September 16, 2008) pgs.1353-1355.

(12) Friedman M., (2003), "Nutritional consequences of food processing," Forum Nutr. 56 (2003) pgs. 350-2.

gratitude

One more thing…

In our lives and in our work, we believe in leading with gratitude. We give heartfelt thanks to all the amazing people who shared their talent and insights in helping us bring The Baby Cuisine Cookbook to life. Special thanks to our families and friends for their love, support, babysitting, and recipe-testing along the way. A very special thank you to Dr. Tamara Cullen, Jessica Peterson of One Tree Photography, Eric Wyttenbach of Ewyttdesign, Lisa Samuel of TCC Printing and Imaging, and all the beautiful babies featured, you all made these pages come to life!

We also thank Keekaroo Highchairs for believing in Alina's Cucina early on – it is our favorite highchair!

Keekaroo® keeps the safety of children in mind when designing the Eco-Friendly Wooden Height Right™ High Chair. Using a renewable natural resource and finishes with low VOC's and pigments helps Keekaroo stay Green.

Keekaroo offers peace of mind to parents, with the style and function necessary for the perfect dining experience for children. Enhance your child's mealtime with Green products from Keekaroo! Grow with Keekaroo and help protect the environment. Visit Keekaroo today! www.keekaroo.com

biography

Shane Valentine

Shane is founder, CEO and "the man behind the mixing bowls" at Alina's Cucina. Well before his daughter, Alina, was born, Shane knew he wanted to carry on the family tradition of making homemade baby food from scratch. After his research turned up less than inspiring options and information, he decided to create his own recipes and infuse them with wholesome ingredients, flavor, and international flair.

As his enthusiasm grew, it became clear that a handful of recipes wouldn't contain his vision. So, he "stirred up" his culinary arts education and years of corporate training experience with a passion for helping others and committed to sharing his vision with the world. The result is Alina's Cucina, which Shane founded in 2008 with his wife, Chantal. They live in Seattle, WA with their daughter, Alina.

Dr. Tamara Cullen, ND

Dr. Cullen plays a key role at Alina's Cucina as the Chief Medical Advisor. She reviews all recipes and ensures that the ingredients and methods are safe and sound for babies and toddlers.

While always feeling an affinity towards women's healthcare, Dr. Cullen began to feel a strong calling toward pediatrics after having her son, Max. She began to realize that by teaching healthy habits of care to children from the earliest age, she could make the biggest difference in the world.

Dr. Cullen is a licensed Naturopathic Physician and a 1999 graduate of Bastyr University. Currently, she serves as adjunct faculty at Bastyr University in their Teaching Clinic and as an Instructor of Advanced Pediatrics. Dr. Cullen owns and practices at Naturopathic Family Medicine located in Seattle, Washington.